Make a Wish

COVER
ILLUSTRATOR

Spotlight

David McPhail

■ David McPhail has drawn many illustrations for children's books. You will find some right here in this book. He says that his best paintings are not planned—they just happen.

■ In the painting on this book cover, he has created a make-believe world. It makes children dream of places long ago and far away. Imagine flying with the children in that wonderful chair!

Acknowledgments appear on page 208, which constitutes an extension of this copyright page.

© 1993 Silver Burdett Ginn Inc.
Cover art © 1993 by David McPhail.

ISBN 0-663-54649-4

1 2 3 4 5 6 7 8 9 10 VHP 98 97 96 95 94 93 92

New Dimensions
IN THE
WORLD OF READING

Make a Wish

PROGRAM AUTHORS

James F. Baumann	Roselmina Indrisano	P. David Pearson
Theodore Clymer	Dale D. Johnson	Taffy E. Raphael
Carl Grant	Connie Juel	Marian Davies Toth
Elfrieda H. Hiebert	Jeanne R. Paratore	Richard L. Venezky

SILVER BURDETT GINN

NEEDHAM, MA   MORRISTOWN, NJ

ATLANTA, GA   DALLAS, TX   DEERFIELD, IL   MENLO PARK, CA

Unit 1 Theme

All About Animals

Unit 2 Theme

Let's # Pretend

All About Animals

Some animals are real, and some are make-believe.

Why do we like stories about animals?

CAROUSEL HORSE, *wood carving by Illions, American, c. 1923*

Theme Books for All About Animals

There are so many different kinds of animals. Do you have a favorite?

❋ Read *If You Give a Moose a Muffin* by Laura Joffe Numeroff to see how messy a hungry moose can be!

❋ In *Over in the Meadow* by Paul Galdone, you can see how different animal families enjoy a sunny day.

❋ What is worse than an octopus with sore feet? You can read *Silly Animal Riddles* by Lisa Eisenberg to find out.

❋ Can you find the animals in *See What You Can See* by Beverley Deitz?

❋ When Aunt Hen is away, the fox tries to catch the lazy hens in *The Chickens, the Crow, and the Fox* by Lisa Eisenberg.

❋ See who drew blue zigzags on a zebra in *Who Painted the Porcupine Purple?* by Lael Littke.

Who Took the Farmer's Hat?

by Joan Nödset

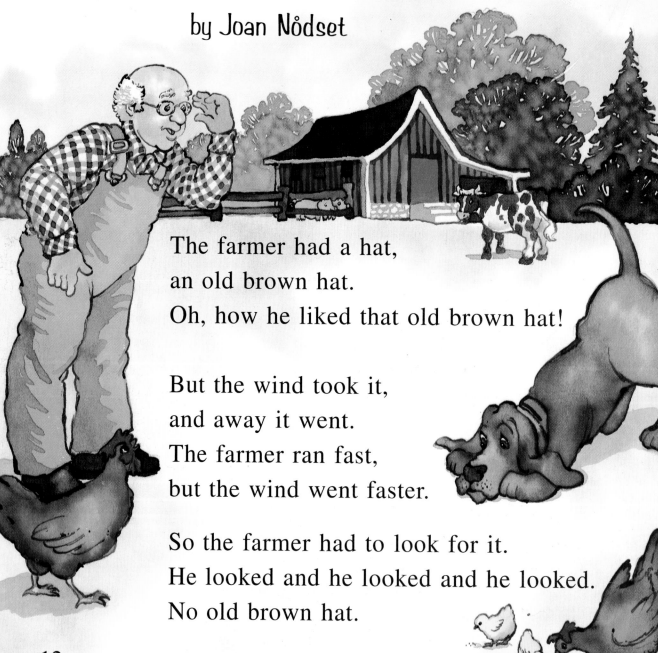

The farmer had a hat,
an old brown hat.
Oh, how he liked that old brown hat!

But the wind took it,
and away it went.
The farmer ran fast,
but the wind went faster.

So the farmer had to look for it.
He looked and he looked and he looked.
No old brown hat.

12

He saw Squirrel.
"Squirrel, did you see
my old brown hat?" said the farmer.

"No," said Squirrel.
"I saw a fat round brown bird in the sky.
A bird with no wings."

The farmer saw Mouse.
"Mouse, did you see
my old brown hat?" said the farmer.

"No," said Mouse.
"I saw a big round brown mousehole
in the grass.
I ran to it, but away it went."

The farmer saw Fly.
"Fly, did you see
my old brown hat?"
said the farmer.

"No," said Fly.
"I saw a flat round brown hill.
The hill was in a tree.
And then that hill took off,
and away it went."

The farmer saw Goat.
"Goat, did you see
my old brown hat?" said the farmer.

"No," said Goat.
"I saw a funny round brown flowerpot.
I was going to eat it,
but the wind took that flowerpot away."

The farmer saw Duck. "Duck, did you see my old brown hat?" said the farmer.

"No," said Duck.
"I saw a silly round brown boat, but Bird took that."

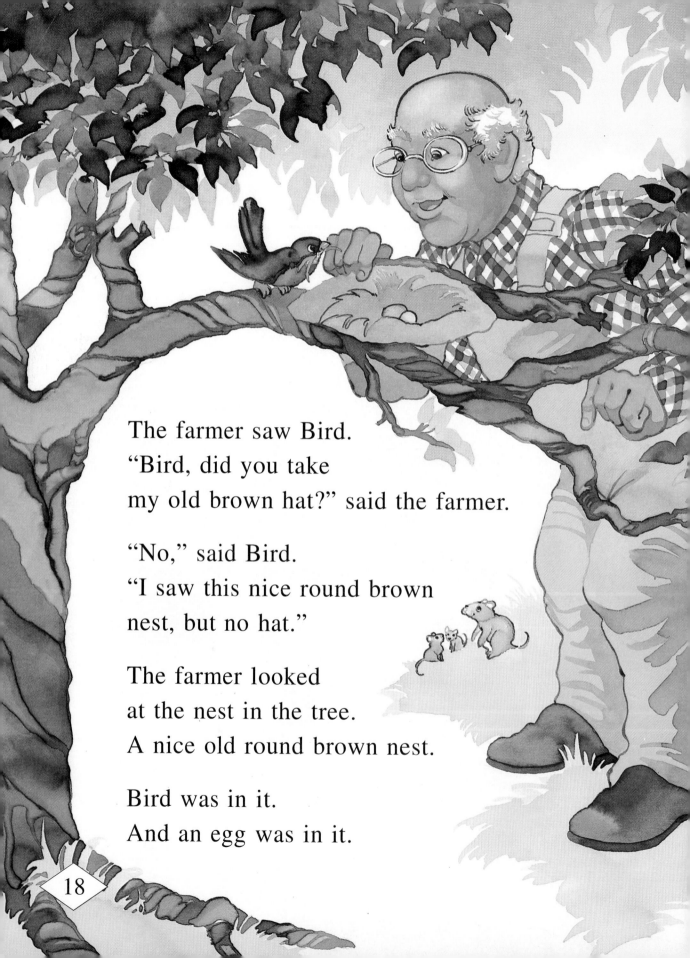

The farmer saw Bird.
"Bird, did you take
my old brown hat?" said the farmer.

"No," said Bird.
"I saw this nice round brown
nest, but no hat."

The farmer looked
at the nest in the tree.
A nice old round brown nest.

Bird was in it.
And an egg was in it.

"Oh, my!" said the farmer.

"Like it?" said Bird.

"I like it," said the farmer.
"Oh, yes, I like that nice round brown nest.
It looks a *little* like my old brown hat.
But I see it is a nice round brown nest."

The farmer has a new brown hat.
Oh, how he likes that new brown hat!
And how Bird likes that old brown nest!

Reader's Response ～ Pretend you are
the farmer's dog. What does the farmer's
hat look like to you?

Library Link ～ *Look in your library for
more books by Joan Nödset. She wrote*
Come Here, Cat *and* Go Away, Dog.

What Do You See?

In the story, a hat looks like other things. Did you know that some insects stay safe because they look like other things?

This insect is a moth. The colors on its back look like a wasp. Animals don't want to eat a wasp, so the moth stays safe.

What do you see here? These are other insects called thorn bugs. They look like thorns on a tree. Birds are fooled and don't want to eat them.

A Morning in Fall

by Reeve Lindbergh

This is the farm on a morning in fall.
The sun has come over the hill.
Come and see who is sleeping and who is awake,
When the farm in the morning looks still.

23

Puppies will sleep this morning in fall.

Puppies sleep late on the farm.

One sleeping brother stays close to his mother.

It makes him feel happy and warm.

The cat is not sleeping this morning in fall.
The cat sees the cows going out.
She likes the warm sun on a morning that's fun.
She likes to be up and about.

Cows are not sleeping this morning in fall.
In the morning the cows go outside.

Take a calf for a run
    and have all kinds of fun.
Take him back to his
    warm mother's side.

Sheep are not sleeping this
    morning in fall.
You can run with the
    sheep down the hill.
You may find one sheep who
    is so good and so kind,
When you give her a hug
    she stays still.

Pigs are not sleeping this morning in fall.
Pigs like to play in the sun.
They play with their mother and play with
  each other.
These pigs all want to have fun.

This is the farm on a morning in fall,
When the sun has come over the hill.
You have seen who is sleeping and
  who is awake,
When the farm in the morning looks still.

Reader's Response ∼ What noises do
you think you would hear on this farm in the
morning in fall?

Chewing, Chewing, Chewing

These cows are eating grass,
which they will turn into milk.

First, a cow chews grass and swallows it.
But the grass is not ready to leave her
stomach. She must bring it back and chew
it some more. To eat this way, a cow has
a special stomach. Sheep, goats, and deer
have the same kind. If you see one of
these animals chewing and chewing,
you'll know why.

A Rainbow for Sara

by Jane Mechling

illustrated by Floyd Cooper

Sara sat and sat, looking out at the big tree. She looked at her mother and asked, "Mom, do you have some string?"

"Yes, here is some red string," said Sara's mother. "Is it for your hair?"

"No," said Sara. "It's not for my hair."

"I know," said Mother. "You're going to fix something with it."

"No," said Sara. "You'll see."

Sara saw that her father had some
string, too. She asked him for it.

"Here you are," said her father.
"Do you need it to put around a box?"

"No," said Sara. "You'll see."

"I know," said Father. "You're
going to fly your kite with it."

"No," Sara said. "I'm thinking
of something else."

Sara ran outside to play with
Peter and Anna.

"I'm keeping string in a box,"
said Sara.

"I have some green string in my
pocket. You may have it," said Peter.

"You're keeping string?"
said Anna. "What are you going
to do with all that string? Will
you and your cat play with it?"

"No," said Sara. "You'll see."

Soon Sara had all the string
she needed. She had red string, orange
string, green string, and yellow string.
She had purple string, too! Sara put
all her string near the big tree
and waited.

She waited and waited. Then she
waited some more. She waited until it
was time for bed.

In the morning, Sara's mom asked, "Where is all your string?"

"Come with me," said Sara. She got her dad, and Peter and Anna, too.

37

"Look!" said Sara.

"Oh my!" said Sara's dad.
"Your string helped a bird make
her nest."

Sara's mother said, "And look!
The bird made a rainbow for Sara!"

Reader's Response ～ How would
you help birds make a nest?

Building a Nest

Birds build nests in [tree]s, on cliffs, or

in [barn]s.

Have you ever seen a [bird] make a [nest]?

[bird]s use [twig], [yarn], or mud to make their

[nest]s. A [duck] uses its own [feathers] to make its

nest soft.

[nest] can be big or small. The nest of a

hummingbird is as small as a baby's [hand]. An

eagle made the biggest [nest] ever seen. It was as

heavy as a [car]!

When You Talk to a Monkey

When you talk to a monkey,
   He seems very wise.
He scratches his head,
   And he blinks both his eyes;
But he won't say a word.
   He just swings on a rail
And makes a big question mark
   Out of his tail.

Rowena Bennett

The
Three Little Pigs

by Adam Burdick

PLAYERS

Peddler 1   Pig 1   Wolf

Peddler 2   Pig 2

Peddler 3   Pig 3

Peddler 1: Straw! Straw for sale!
One corncob for a bale!

Peddler 2: Get your sticks! Just cut!
Sticks for sale!

Peddler 3: Bricks! Just six corncobs.

Pig 1: I think I'll make my house
from straw. Straw is strong.
Please give me some straw.

Pig 2: I think I'll make my house
from sticks. Sticks are
stronger than straw. Please
give me some sticks.

Pig 3: And I'll make my house from
bricks. Bricks cost more,
but they are the strongest
of all. Please give me
some bricks.

Pig 1: What a fine house
I've made.

Wolf: Knock, knock.

Pig 1: Who is it?

Wolf: It's a friend. Little pig,
little pig, please, let me in.

Pig 1: Not by the hair on my
chinny chin chin.

Wolf: Then I'll huff and I'll puff,
and I'll blow your house in!

Pig 1: Help! Help! The wolf is
here. I'll run to my
sister's house. Her stick house
will keep me safe.

Pig 1:   Sister, Sister, please, let me in!
         The wolf blew my house down!

Pig 2:   Come in, come in. My house
         of sticks will keep you safe.

Wolf: Knock, knock.

Pig 2:   Who is it?

Wolf: It's a friend. Little pig,
little pig, please, let me in.

Pigs 1 & 2: Not by the hairs on our
chinny chin chins.

Wolf: Then I'll huff, and I'll puff,
and I'll blow your house in!

Pig 2: We can run to our big sister's
house. Her brick house will
keep us safe.

47

Pigs 1 & 2: Knock, knock.

Pig 3: Can I help you?

Pig 1: The wolf blew down
my straw house.

Pig 2: The wolf blew down
my stick house.

Pigs 1 & 2: Can we come in with you?

Pig 3: Come in, come in. You'll
be safe in my strong
brick house.

Wolf: Knock, knock.

Pig 3: Who is it?

Wolf: It's a friend. Little pig,
little pig, please, let me in.

Pigs 1, 2, Not by the hairs on our
and 3: chinny chin chins.

Wolf: Then I'll huff, and I'll puff,
and I'll blow your house in.

Pig 3: My house is too strong.
        You cannot blow it in.

Wolf: Huff, puff! Huff, puff!
        Huff, puff! Huff, puff!
        Just one more time will
        blow this house down!
        HUFFFFFFF, PUFFFFFF.
        Oh, I give up! This house
        is too strong!

Reader's Response ⌒ Would you like to
live in a house made from straw or sticks?
Tell why.

Masks

Long, long ago people started making masks. And people all over the world still make masks from wood, beads, and feathers. The masks look like animals, fish, and birds.

Here is a mask that looks like the sun. It was made by Native Americans from the Northwest Coast. Adults wear masks like this one to sing and dance and tell stories. They use the masks to act out animal tales and other stories from the tribe's past.

Why would you make a mask?

BELLA COOLA WOODEN SUN MASK. (Photo by Stephen S. Myers).
Courtesy, Department of Library Service, American Museum of Natural History.

51

Under a STONE

by Aileen Fisher

In the middle of a meadow
we turned up a stone
and saw a little village
we never had known,
with little streets and tunnels
and ant-folk on the run,
all frightened and excited
by the sudden burst of sun.

We watched them rushing headlong,
and then put back the stone
to cover up the village
we never had known,
to roof away the tunnels
where ants were on the run . . .
before they got all sunburned
in the bright hot sun.

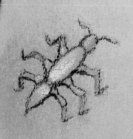

A World of Animals

by Susan Schroeder

The world is home for many animals.
All animals need a place to live.

You can find animals under the
ground, in the sky, and in the water.
Animals live all around us.

Turtles live on land and in water.
All turtles have a shell. The shell is
a home for the turtle. Some turtles can
hide in their shells.

Ducks make their homes near water. Ducks swim in the water and look for food. They make nests out of grass and mud near the water. The grass around the water hides their nests.

Some rabbits make their homes in meadows. They dig holes under the ground. Then they make nests out of their fur. Under the ground, the rabbits are warm and safe.

Many birds make their homes
in trees. They fly to the ground
to find things for their nests. They
take the grass, sticks, and mud to
the trees to make their nests. Birds
are safe in their homes in the trees.

All animals need a place to
live. There are many animal homes
in the world. Look around you.
What animals live near you?

Reader's Response ～ How would you
like to live in a turtle's home? Tell how it
would feel.

A Web is a Home

Turtles have shells, and birds have nests. But where do spiders live? Some live on leaves. Others dig tunnels to live in. Many spiders spin simple webs. Others spin webs of different shapes.

Do you see the circles in this web? This web is called an orb. Have you ever seen one?

Here is another web. What shape is it? Does it look like a triangle?

Snail

They have brought me a snail.

Inside it sings
a map-green ocean.
My heart
swells with water,
with small fish
of brown and silver.

They have brought me a snail.

Federico García Lorca

Caracola

Me han traído una caracola.

Dentro le canta
un mar de mapa.
Mi corazón
se llena de agua,
con pececillos
de sombra y plata.

Me han traído una caracola.

Federico García Lorca

63

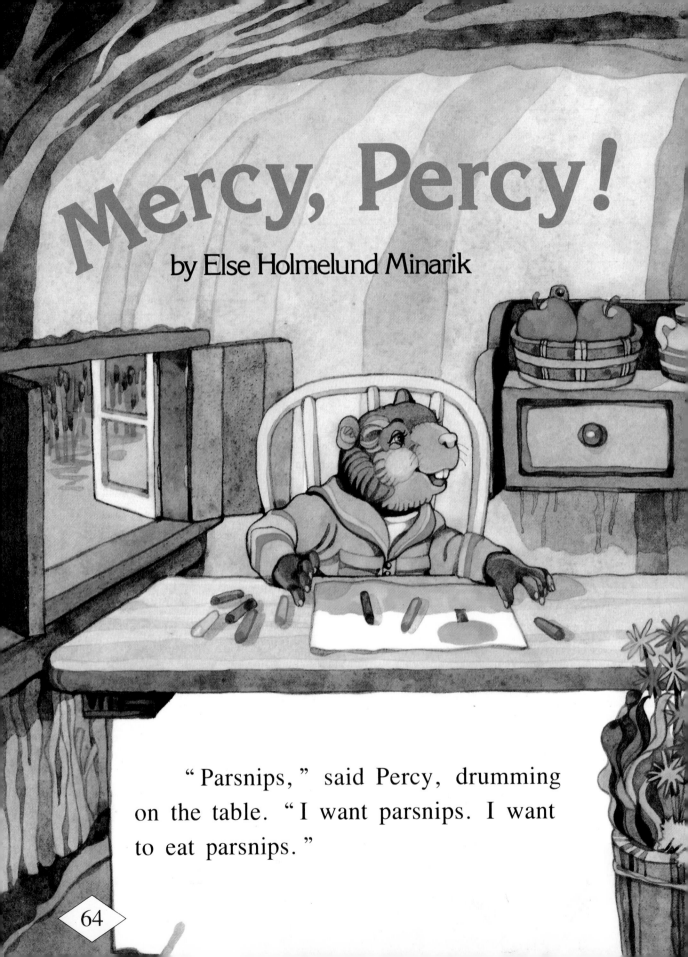

Mercy, Percy!

by Else Holmelund Minarik

"Parsnips," said Percy, drumming on the table. "I want parsnips. I want to eat parsnips."

"Mother," said Percy. "Will you cook parsnips for me?"

"Mercy, Percy!" said Mother. "We have no parsnips. Will bark bits do?"

65

No, Percy did not want bark bits.
Percy wanted parsnips.

"I want parsnips," said Percy.
He drummed on the table.

"Stop drumming on the table!" said Mother. "Here is your grandpa."

"Grandpa, Percy wants to eat parsnips. I have no parsnips. Do you have any parsnips?" said Mother.

67

"Oh, yes!" said Grandpa. "I have fine parsnips in my garden. My parsnips are the best! Come with me, Percy. We'll get the parsnips. Then we can help Mother cook them for you."

They came to the garden. Percy
looked about. He saw some strawberries.
He ate them.

And he saw some gooseberries,
some big fine gooseberries. He began
to eat the gooseberries.

69

Now gooseberry bushes are sticky.
But that did not stop Percy.

"I like it here," said Percy.
"I like to be stuck in sticky bushes,
with big fine gooseberries to eat."

Percy ate a lot of gooseberries.

Grandpa pulled up his parsnips. And then he pulled Percy out of the bushes.

"Percy," said Grandpa, "you'll have a gooseberry tummy ache."

Grandpa was right. Percy did have
a gooseberry tummy ache.

Percy cried, "All I wanted was
parsnips!"

Mother said, "Parsnips will have to
wait." She patted Percy's tummy.

Percy waited.

Then he was fine. His tummy ache went away.

"I'm fine now, Mother," he said. "I'm ready for parsnips."

"Good for you," said Mother.

She cooked the parsnips and Percy ate them.

"Mercy, Percy!" said Mother. "Do you want more?"

"Yes," said Percy.

"I'll have some too," said Grandpa.

Mother said, "Well then, so will I."

So they had a family parsnip party!

Percy did not get a parsnip tummy ache. Not Percy! But then, no one ever gets a parsnip tummy ache.

Reader's Response ∼ What do you think Percy will do when he goes into the garden tomorrow?

About Beavers

The animals in this story are make-believe beavers. Real beavers build their homes in streams or lakes. They use mud and sticks. They cut down the trees all by themselves.

Beavers are great swimmers. Even four-day-old babies can swim. Beavers can hold their breath for over five minutes under the water.

To warn its family about danger, a beaver smacks its tail on the water.

What a splash that would make!

EZRA JACK KEATS

WHISTLE
FOR WILLIE

Oh, how Peter wished he could whistle!

He saw a boy playing with his dog.
Whenever the boy whistled,
the dog ran straight to him.

Peter tried and tried to whistle,
but he couldn't. So instead
he began to turn himself around—
around and around he whirled . . .
faster and faster . . .

When he stopped
everything turned
down . . .
and up . . .
and up . . .
and down . . .
and around
and
around.

Peter saw his dog, Willie, coming.
Quick as a wink, he hid in an empty
carton lying on the sidewalk.

"Wouldn't it be funny if I whistled?"
Peter thought. "Willie would stop
and look all around to see who it was."

Peter tried again to whistle — but still he
couldn't. So Willie just walked on.

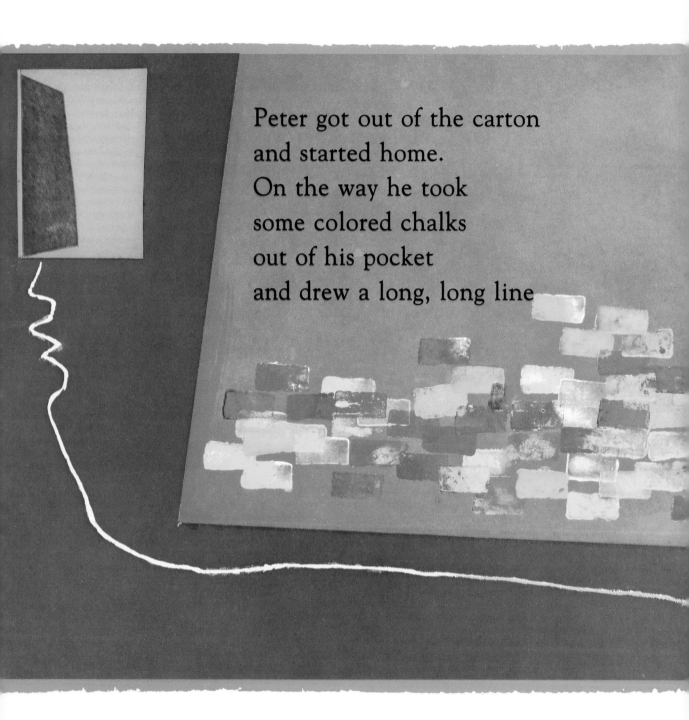

Peter got out of the carton
and started home.
On the way he took
some colored chalks
out of his pocket
and drew a long, long line

right up to his door.
He stood there and tried to whistle again.
He blew till his cheeks were tired.
But nothing happened.

He went into his house and put on his
father's old hat to make himself feel more
grown-up. He looked into the mirror to
practice whistling.
Still
no
whistle!

When his mother saw what he was doing,
Peter pretended that he was his father.
He said, "I've come home early today, dear.
Is Peter here?"

His mother answered,
"Why no, he's outside with Willie."
"Well, I'll go out and look for them," said Peter.

First he walked along a crack in the sidewalk.
Then he tried to run away from his shadow.

He jumped off his shadow
But when he landed
they were
together
again.

He came to the corner
where the carton was,
and who should he see but Willie!

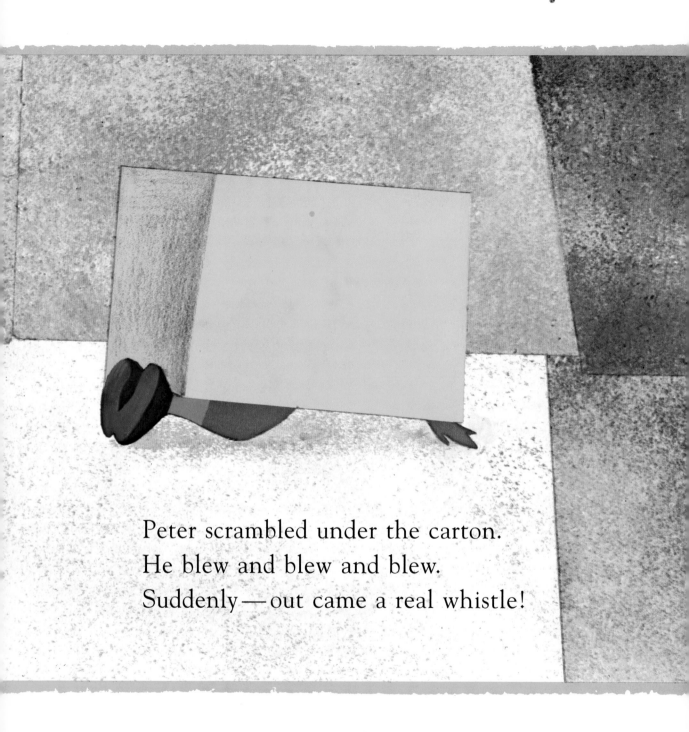

Peter scrambled under the carton.
He blew and blew and blew.
Suddenly—out came a real whistle!

Willie stopped and looked around to see
who it was.

"It's me," Peter shouted, and stood up.
Willie raced straight to him.

Peter ran home
to show his father and mother what he could
do. They loved Peter's whistling. So did Willie.

Peter's mother asked him and Willie
to go on an errand to the grocery store.

He whistled all the way there,
and he whistled all the way home.

Reader's Response 〜 Pretend you
are Peter. How would you feel when you
learned to whistle?

Let's Pretend

Pretend

Sometimes it's fun to pretend.
How can a story help you pretend?

FRENCH TIN TOYS, c. 1898

Theme Books for
Let's Pretend

Just pretend—and anything can happen!

※ When Peter wakes up, snow covers everything! Follow Peter through his special day in *The Snowy Day* by Ezra Jack Keats.

※ Bear will learn to fly if he can teach Little Bird to be big. What happens in *Bear's Bargain* by Frank Asch?

* Leopard and Zebra can't agree in *A Stripe and a Spot* by Julie Small-Gamby and Gail Tuchman.

* Meet Nick's make-believe friend in *Otto's Tricks* by Ethan Miles.

* In *Unicorn Seems to Have Lost Its Hat* by Gail Tuchman, everyone has a hat. But what about Unicorn?

* Race with giants in *The Best Place for Imagining* by Marjorie Weinman.

The Wishing Well

from *Mouse Tales*

written and illustrated
by ARNOLD LOBEL

A mouse once found
a wishing well.
"Now all of my wishes
can come true!"
she cried.
She threw a penny
into the well
and made a wish.
"OUCH!"
said the wishing well.

The next day
the mouse came back
to the well.
She threw a penny
into the well
and made a wish.
"OUCH!" said the well.

The next day
the mouse came back again.
She threw a penny
into the well.
"I wish this well
would not say ouch,"
she said.
"OUCH!" said the well.
"That hurts!"

" What shall I do? "
cried the mouse.
" My wishes
will never ever
come true this way! "

The mouse ran home.
She took the pillow
from her bed.
"This may help,"
said the mouse,
and she ran back
to the well.

The mouse threw the pillow
into the well.
Then she threw
a penny into the well
and made a wish.

" Ah . That feels
much better! "
said the well.
" Good! " said the mouse.
" Now I can start wishing . "

After that day
the mouse made many wishes
by the well.
And every one of them
came true.

Reader's Response ∿ How would
you have solved the mouse's problem?

A Lucky Cricket?

Have you ever had a wish come true? Did that make you feel lucky? People all over the world have different ideas about what is lucky.

Have you heard of these ideas? In China people think the number 8 is lucky. In some countries people think it's lucky to find a cricket in the house. Many people think a four-leaf clover is lucky.

What do you think is lucky?

Last Saturday
I was eating breakfast,
when all of a sudden
a tyrannosaurus
came crashing through
the window.

And Peggy said . . .

When I got to
Jimmy's house
for breakfast,
there was
a tyrannosaurus
at the table.
It was eating up
all the eggs,
and there were broken dishes
all over the floor.

And Susan said . . .

I was going over
to Jimmy's too,
But when I got there,
a tyrannosaurus
was stuck on the stairs
and Peggy and Jimmy
were yelling for help.

And Billy said . . .

I was on my way
to the store and I heard
a yell from Jimmy's house.
So I ran across the street
and there were Jimmy
and Peggy and Susan
and a big tyrannosaurus
stuck on the stairs.
We all pulled and pushed and
pushed and pulled, but suddenly,
the tyrannosaurus sneezed and
we were blown out the door.

And Alice said . . .

I was waiting for the bus, when Jimmy and Peggy and Susan and Billy and a tyrannosaurus came flying out onto the street.

And Rusty said . . .

124

I was also waiting
for the bus,
and Jimmy and Peggy
and Susan and Billy
and Alice and the tyrannosaurus
and I all squeezed on.
Everyone else
had to get off.

And Stuart said . . .

I was sitting
on the seesaw
at the playground,
and this tyrannosaurus
came running up and
plopped down on the other end
and I flew into the air
and landed on his back.

And Joanne said . . .

I was on the swings,
and Jimmy and Peggy
and all of my friends
came dashing by
with a tyrannosaurus.
And I jumped off
and ran after them.

And Debby said . . .

I was starting
my motorbike
near the playground,
when out raced Jimmy and Peggy
and Susan and Billy and
Alice and Rusty and Stuart
and Joanne and the tyrannosaurus.
And they all jumped on behind me
and we took off for
the amusement park.

And Rachel said . . .

I was walking my dog,
and who should I see
but all the kids from school
running into the amusement park
with a tyrannosaurus.
I ran in after them and
my dog came too.

And Barbara said . . .

I was on the roller coaster, and I turned around and there was a tyrannosaurus with Jimmy and Peggy and Susan and Billy and Alice and Rusty and Stuart and Joanne and Debby and Rachel and Rachel's dog.

And Tommy said . . .

130

I was on the merry-go-round, and the tyrannosaurus came charging past with all my friends and it knocked over the man who takes the tickets and ran away.

And Philip said . . .

TOMMY PHILIP

131

And then
the cops came
and looked all over
the city,
but the tyrannosaurus
was gone!

PHILIP

Reader's Response ⁓ Pretend you
could add on to the story. Where did the
tyrannosaurus go?

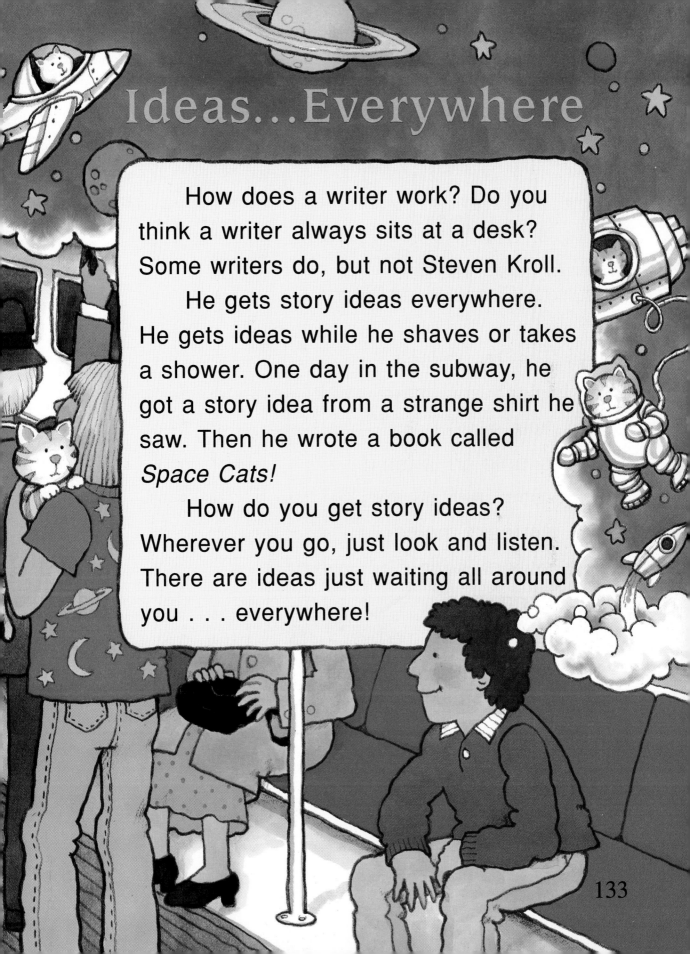

Ideas...Everywhere

How does a writer work? Do you think a writer always sits at a desk? Some writers do, but not Steven Kroll.

He gets story ideas everywhere. He gets ideas while he shaves or takes a shower. One day in the subway, he got a story idea from a strange shirt he saw. Then he wrote a book called *Space Cats!*

How do you get story ideas? Wherever you go, just look and listen. There are ideas just waiting all around you . . . everywhere!

By Myself

written by Eloise Greenfield
illustrated by Diane and Leo Dillon

When I'm by myself
And I close my eyes
I'm a twin
I'm a dimple in a chin
I'm a room full of toys
I'm a squeaky noise
I'm a gospel song
I'm a gong
I'm a leaf turning red
I'm a loaf of brown bread
I'm a whatever I want to be
An anything I care to be
And when I open my eyes
What I care to be
Is me

134

135

Hippo Makes
a Wish

from *Hippo Lemonade*

written by Mike Thaler
illustrated by Maxie Chambliss

Hippo opened his eyes.
"Today I would like
to make a wish," he said.
Hippo thought and thought.
But he could not think of anything
to wish for.

So he got out of the river
and went to see Snake.

"Snake," said Hippo,
"I would like to make a wish.
But I don't know what to wish for."
"Wish for bright colors, like mine,"
said Snake.
Hippo saw himself with bright colors
like Snake's.

"I don't think so," said Hippo.
And he went to see Monkey.

"Wish for a
long tail like
mine," said Monkey.
"Then we could swing
in the trees together."
Hippo saw himself
swinging in the trees.
"I don't think so," he said.
And he went to see Lion.

"Wish for a curly mane
like mine," said Lion.
Hippo saw himself
with a mane like Lion's.

"I don't think so," he said,
and he went to see Giraffe.

"You could see the tops of trees,"
said Giraffe,
"with a neck like mine."
Hippo saw himself
with a long neck like Giraffe's.
"I don't think so," said Hippo,
and he went to see Parrot.

"Feathers!" said Parrot.
"Wish for feathers."

Hippo saw himself
all covered with feathers.
"I don't think so," said Hippo,
and he went to see Elephant.

"I know!" said Elephant.
"Wish for a nose just like mine."

Hippo saw himself
with Elephant's nose.
"I don't think so," he said,
and he went back to the river.

He closed his eyes.

"What are you doing?" asked Mole.

"I am wishing," said Hippo.

"What are you wishing for?"
asked Mole.

"I am wishing to stay
just as I am," said Hippo.
Mole looked at Hippo.
Hippo looked at Mole.
Mole winked.
"Your wish has come true."

Reader's Response ∼ What would
you have told Hippo to wish for if you
had been his friend?

ANANSI
THE SPIDER

One day Anansi, the wise and tricky spider, said to his friend Rhino, "Let's play tug of war."

"Sure," smiled Rhino. He was sure he could beat a small spider.

So Anansi gave one end of a rope to Rhino. He ran over the hill, gave the other end to Hippo, and said, "Let's play tug of war."

"OK," laughed Hippo.

Then Anansi ran to the top of the hill. Hippo and Rhino could see Anansi, but not each other.

"Pull!" shouted the spider.

Rhino pulled. Hippo pulled. Each could not move the other. Anansi didn't pull. He was too busy laughing.

147

Scramble

If the zebra were given
  the spots of the leopard
and the leopard
  the stripes of the zebra,
then the leopard would have to
  be renamed the zeopard,
and the zebra retitled the lebra.

And wouldn't we laugh
  if the gentle giraffe
swapped his neck for the
  hump on the camel?
For the camel would henceforth
  be called the camaffe,
the giraffe designated giramel.

148

It would be very funny,
    if the ears of the bunny
were exchanged for
    the horns of the sheep.
For the sheep would then surely
    be known as the shunny,
and the bunny quite simply the beep.

Jack Prelutsky

David McPhail

David McPhail makes picture books. He makes up the story and the drawings, too.

"I started to draw when I was two," Mr. McPhail said. "I drew pictures on brown bags. I drew pictures on anything I could find at home and at school."

Mr. McPhail said, "My mother liked my drawings a lot. She would hang them up around the house. My mother told my sister and brothers that we could be anything we wanted to be!"

Mr. McPhail has a house in New England. "I like books, tall trees, the warm sun, and the blue sky," he said. "I don't like snow, ice, and TV."

"I always have new stories in my mind," Mr. McPhail said. "When I sit in my car, I may think of anything. I may think of a pig in a truck. I may think of bears."

"One time I wanted to make a picture book about a bear. I made many drawings of bears," said Mr. McPhail.

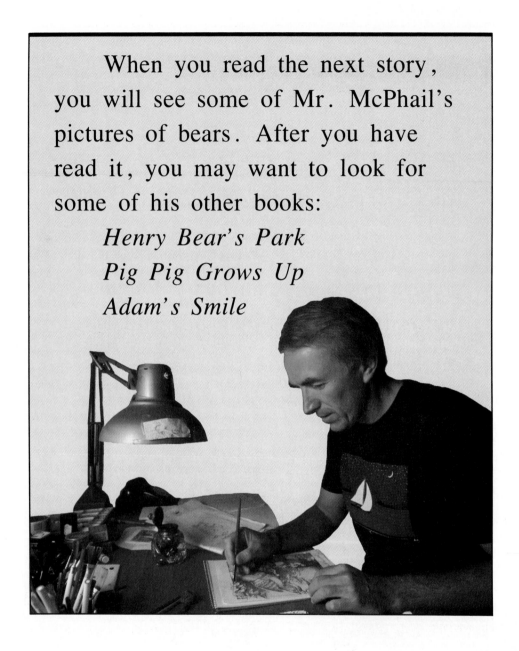

When you read the next story, you will see some of Mr. McPhail's pictures of bears. After you have read it, you may want to look for some of his other books:

Henry Bear's Park
Pig Pig Grows Up
Adam's Smile

Reader's Response ∿ David McPhail likes to draw pictures. What do you like to do?

A Young Artist

Wang Yani was born in China. Like David McPhail, she began to paint when she was two. She soon became famous. A large museum in the United States asked her to send some of her paintings so that people there could see them, too.

Wang Yani likes to put herself in her paintings. But she doesn't paint a girl. She paints herself as a monkey! If you painted yourself as an animal, what would you be?

FIX-IT

written and illustrated
by David McPhail

One morning Emma got up
early to watch television.
But the TV didn't work.

Emma asked her mother to fix it.
"Hurry, Mom!" she cried.
Emma's mother tried to fix it.
But she couldn't.

Emma's father tried.
But he couldn't fix it, either.
So he called the fix-it man.
"Please hurry," he said.
"It's an emergency!"

The fix-it man came right away.
He tried to fix the TV.
Emma's mother and father
tried to fix Emma.
Her father blew up a balloon . . .
until it popped.

Her mother sang a song.
So did the cat.
Her father pretended to be a horse—
but Emma didn't feel like riding.

Finally her mother read her a book.
"Read it again," said Emma
when her mother had finished.
"And again."
"And again."

"Now *I'll* read to Millie,"
said Emma.
And she went to her room.

Then her father found out what was
wrong with the TV.
"I fixed it!" he called.
But Emma didn't come out of her room.

She was too busy.

Reader's Response ⁓ What kinds of
books can keep you busy all day?

164

A Rainy Day Box

Emma had fun without TV. Could you? Here's how one child had fun in the days before there was TV.

"My mother had a rainy day box. In it she kept old buttons, scraps of pretty paper and cloth, paints, and crayons. When it rained, she took out the box. Sometimes we made something out of what was in the box. Other times she told us stories about what she saved. One of the buttons was from a shirt my dad wore when he was a pilot."

The Trouble With Elephants

written and illustrated by

Chris Riddell

The trouble with elephants is . . .
they spill the bathwater when they get in . . .

and they leave a pink elephant ring when they get out.

167

They take all the sheets, and they snore
elephant snores, which rattle the
windowpanes.

The only way to wake a sleeping
elephant is to shout "Mouse!"
in its ear.

Then it will slide down the banister
to breakfast.

Elephants <u>travel</u> four in <u>a car</u>—two in the front and two in <u>the back</u>.

You can <u>always tell</u> when an elephant is
visiting <u>because</u> there'll be a <u>car</u> outside
with <u>three elephants</u> in it.

Sometimes elephants ride bicycles . . .

but not <u>very</u> often.

The trouble with elephants is that on elephant picnics they eat all the cupcakes before you've finished your first one.

Elephants drink their lemonade through their trunks, and if you're not looking, they drink yours too.

On elephant picnics they play games
like leap-elephant and jump rope,
which they're good at.

And sometimes they play <u>hide-and-seek</u>,
which <u>they're</u> not very good at.

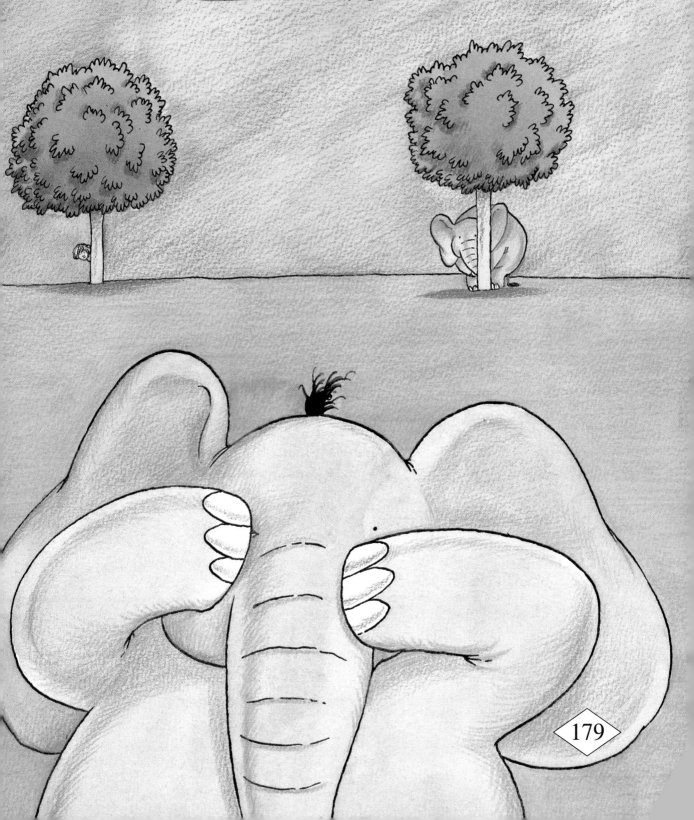

179

The trouble with elephants is . . .
well, there are all sorts of troubles . . .

all <u>sorts</u> of <u>troubles</u> . . .

181

but the <u>real</u> trouble is . . .

you can't help but love them.

Reader's Response ∿ Which of the troubles with elephants did you like best? Tell why.

Glossary

A

Sue loves **animals.**

awake

after Jane helps around the house every day after school.

again It rained every day this week. It will rain again today.

animals Sue loves dogs, cats, birds, and other animals.

anything When he was sick, Sean didn't eat anything all day.

asked Mark asked for help.

awake The baby was awake all night.

away Mary went away for the day.

184

B

balloon Pam bought a green balloon.

began Sue was hungry so she began to eat.

better Jim felt much better after he saw the doctor.

blew The wind blew the man's hat off.

blow Lin will blow out the candles.

boring Sometimes it is boring to play inside all day.

bricks Our house is made from bricks.

bright Red and purple are bright colors.

broken Mom tried to fix the broken wheel on my bike.

brown The house is painted brown.

busy Ernest was busy painting the door.

balloon

blow

broken

C

calf

closed

corncob

curly

calf The cow licked her calf.

cannot The hen cannot find her eggs.

chin Alma has milk on her chin.

chinny Not by the hair on my chinny chin chin.

close Abe lives close to Ruth's house.

closed This shop is closed on Sundays.

colors The drawing has many bright colors in it.

corncob After you eat corn, the corncob is left.

cows These cows give lots of milk.

cried Carole cried when her puppy ran away.

curly My hair is curly, just like Mom's.

186

D

dishes Jason helped wash the dishes.

draw Rick likes to draw trees.

drawings Jane makes drawings of cats with her pencil.

drew Jane drew four cats on her paper.

drumming Percy was drumming his fingers on the table and making very loud noises.

draw

E

eat

early We went to bed early.

eat Bears eat lots of fish.

either I don't want to go either.

else Bob is still hungry. He wants something else to eat.

emergency Call your parents if there is an emergency.

ever Will we ever get to the beach?

emergency

farm

food

friend

every We have a big family picnic every summer.

everyone Everyone in my class likes to read every day.

F

---

farm Carmen saw pigs and hens at the farm.

farmer The farmer lives on the farm.

fast Kim ran very fast.

finally Laura finally finished building the model.

flew The duck flew away.

fly I wish I could fly like a bird.

food The birds have food to eat.

friend Carmen is Juan's best friend.

funny Julian told a funny joke.

fur My cat has very soft fur.

G

---

game The children made up a new game.

garden We like to grow carrots and beans in our garden.

going Mr. Smith is going to work.

gone The rabbits have gone into their hole to sleep.

gooseberries We picked gooseberries from the bushes.

Grandpa Grandpa is my mom's father.

ground Greg planted seeds in the ground.

game

ground

H

---

hair Maria likes to brush her hair.

heard Rob heard the dog bark.

hill Jack and Jill climbed up the hill.

himself José was talking to himself.

house That house is where I live.

hurry Cathy must hurry to catch the bus.

hurts John's sore foot hurts whenever he walks.

hill

hurry

knock

meadows

mouse

mousehole

K

kinds The shop sells many kinds of bread and cheese.

knock Dad began to knock on the door.

L

liked Tom liked his new friend.

M

many There are many animals on my uncle's farm.

meadows The cows were eating grass in the meadows.

Mother Mother likes us to get dressed when we first get up.

mouse The mouse ran under the bed.

mousehole The cat tried to grab the mouse in the mousehole.

N

nest The birds made a nest.

never Alice is never late for school.

new Gail's old coat was too small. She just got a new one.

next The next bus stop is Dave's.

nice Betty made a nice gift for me.

nest

opened

O

old This house has been here for a long time. It is very old.

opened Father opened the letter.

orange Beth picked out a big orange pumpkin.

ouch "Ouch!" said Edward when he cut his finger.

our We live here. This is our house.

outside Mother was in the shop. We waited outside.

orange

parsnips

penny

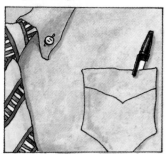

pocket

puppies

P

parsnips Parsnips grow under the ground like carrots.

penny Amy put a penny in her bank.

pictures Clara draws pictures of dogs in art class.

please "Please, can I go out to play?" asked Amanda.

pocket Mr. Long's pen is in his pocket.

pretended Pat pretended she was a tree during the school play.

pulled Robert pulled the wagon up the big hill.

puppies All the puppies are asleep.

purple Sara has a purple dress.

pushed Todd pushed the door open.

R

rabbits Rabbits like to eat carrots.

rainbow You may see a rainbow if it rains as the sun comes out.

read Nan will read to the class today. Bill read yesterday.

riding I see Ted riding his bike.

river We went to the river to go fishing.

round A ball is round.

running The mouse was running from the cat.

rabbits

rainbow

read

river

sheep

Mother reads a **story.**

straw

string

194

S

sheep The sheep are on the hill.

soon It is late. I want to go home soon.

start It is time to start the race.

stays A pine tree stays green all year.

sticks Lee picked up all the sticks in the yard.

sticky My fingers were sticky after eating the ice cream.

still The dentist told Jack to sit still.

stories Joe liked all the stories his father read to him.

straw Cows and horses eat straw.

string Mike tied up the box with string.

strong The strong man lifted the big heavy box.

T

table Jen helped set the table.

television Nancy watches television in the morning.

their We went to see our grandpa and grandma. Their house is far away.

there We went to the beach. It was sunny and warm there.

things I like to make things out of clay.

thinking Harriet was thinking about her new pet.

thought Robin thought of a gift for Tom.

threw Andy threw the ball to his sister.

today Today is Sunday.

together All four of us went to the party together.

told Dad told me about the large birds.

took We took a walk with the dog.

tried Jim tried to catch the bus.

true It is true that ducks can fly.

things

thinking

threw

Dad **told** me.

195

turtles

two pieces

winked

tummy I ate too many apples, and my tummy hurts.

turtles Turtles can swim very well.

two The dish broke into two pieces.

U

under Ron sleeps under the blankets.

until We can play until it gets dark.

W

waited We waited for our dog Annie to come home.

warm The sun feels warm.

when The dog barks when we come home each day.

where I live here. Where do you live?

winked Joan winked at her brother as she told the joke.

world The ship sailed around the world.

would Anna has a big sandwich. She
would like to share it with Jeff.

wrong When Dad took a wrong turn, he
lost his way.

world

Y

---

yellow The color of our fence is bright
yellow.

Anna **would** like
to share.

yellow fence

197

ABOUT THE
Authors & *Illustrators*

Rowena Bennett

Rowena Bennett's poems and plays
are about animals, people, and the
world around us. Her poems are
part of collections of poetry. Her
writing is enjoyed by many readers.

Floyd Cooper

Floyd Cooper designed cards, like birthday cards, before he started to illustrate children's books. The first book he illustrated, *Grandpa's Face*, won several awards. He likes to draw different people in a family, from children to grandparents. He likes his work very much and likes the creativity that being a book illustrator provides.

Diane and Leo Dillon

Leo and Diane Dillon met while they were in art school. Since that time they have worked together to illustrate many books for children and adults. They have won several awards, including the Caldecott Medal for their illustrations in *Why Mosquitoes Buzz in People's Ears*. They use different art media such as watercolors, paints, pen and ink, and wood cuts in their work.

Aileen Fisher

Aileen Fisher has written many
poems and stories for which she
has won several awards. She grew
up in the country and has always
loved country living. Now she lives
in Colorado near a mountain. She
likes to take a walk with her dog
along the mountain trails.

Eloise Greenfield

Eloise Greenfield did not think she would be a writer when she grew up. She says, "I loved words, but I loved to read them, not write them. I loved their sounds." Now writing is an important part of her life. Eloise Greenfield has received many awards including the American Library Association Notable Book Award.

Ezra Jack Keats

Ezra Jack Keats wrote and illustrated many books. He began painting when he was about four years old. Ezra Jack Keats won many awards for his work.

Steven Kroll

Steven Kroll says, "I really love writing for children." When he writes, he tries to remember things about his own childhood. "When I write about a child's room, that room is often my own." He thinks it is important for writers to remember what it was like to be a young child.

Arnold Lobel

Arnold Lobel wrote and illustrated books for children. His books have won many awards. One thing he especially liked about being a writer was being able to make a character do what *he* wanted to do.

Federico García Lorca

Federico García Lorca was born in Spain. He wrote many poems and stories. Some of the poems were written for children. When he and his sister were little, they liked to hear the stories their nursemaid told them. He liked playing make-believe with disguises and masks. He often used memories from his childhood when he wrote his poetry!

David McPhail

David McPhail illustrates books for children. He also writes books. David McPhail says he does not know what a picture will look like when he begins to draw it. "I have the feeling that if I could see very clearly what I wanted from the beginning, there would be no reason for me to draw." He is a Caldecott winner.

Joan Nödset

Joan Nödset has written many books for children. She gets her ideas for her stories from different places. The idea for one of her books came from a dream she had. When she was growing up, her mother read to her almost every night. Joan Nödset says she wanted to be a writer for as long as she can remember.

Jack Prelutsky

Jack Prelutsky has written many books and poems for children. He was born in New York City where he went to the High School for Music and Art. He sings opera and has worked as a singer, actor, and poet. His poems for children are clever and funny. He writes about people that he knows and also about himself.

Mike Thaler

Mike Thaler has written more than sixty children's books. He also illustrates books. Some of his books are collections of riddles, jokes, and cartoons. Mike Thaler is also a songwriter and a sculptor.

AUTHOR INDEX

208